# ZERO-BASE BUDGETING IN COLLEGES AND UNIVERSITIES

*A Concise Guide to Understanding and Implementing ZBB in Higher Education*

**L. James Harvey, Ph.D.**
**Director of the Education Division**
**McManis Associates, Inc.**
**Washington, D.C.**

**Published by:**

**Ireland Educational Corporation**
2275 East Arapahoe Road, Suite 313
Littleton, Colorado 80122

L. James Harvey, Ph.D.
McManis Associates, Inc.
1201 Connecticut Avenue, N.W.
Washington, D.C.  20036
Telephone:  (202) 296-1355

Library of Congress Catalogue Card Number: 77-075520
International Standard Book Number: 0-89103-017-4

First Edition

# TABLE OF CONTENTS

# TABLE OF TABLES

# PREFACE

The intense pressures for more effective management of our colleges and universities have brought forth a number of management systems. Management by Objective, Planning-Programming-Budgeting Systems and Management Information Systems have become familiar terms in educational management circles. The latest systems approach is Zero-Base Budgeting (ZBB), a concept brought to forefront by President Carter. After using ZBB successfully in the State Government of Georgia, the President is now attempting to implement this approach in the Federal government. ZBB is a system that has merit and relevance for education as well as for government.

In this book Dr. L. James Harvey, Director of our Education Division, has anticipated the need for bringing this concept to educational managers who are interested in the possible use of Zero-Base Budgeting in their colleges and universities. This book presents a brief, clear, concise overview of ZBB for the busy administrator, trustee, faculty member, graduate student or other interested reader. The objectives are to assist the reader in:

- Developing a current knowledge of ZBB;

- Understanding how to implement ZBB; and

- Understanding the linkages of ZBB to other management systems.

Dr. Harvey's extensive experience working with colleges and universities in implementing management systems and his thorough background knowledge of budgeting systems uniquely qualifies him to write on this subject.

Gerald L. McManis
President, McManis Associates, Inc.

i

## AUTHOR'S COMMENT

A number of people have been helpful in putting this publication together. I would like to thank Mr. Robert Listou, Dr. Clifford Berg, Mr. Willard Olson, Mr. William Parker, Dr. Charles Kinnison, and Mr. Edward Robertson, for their critical reviews of the manuscript.

I am also very appreciative of the excellent editorial work by Ms. Lucy Shipe, as well as the typing and publishing assistance of Ms. Mary Zotta and her staff.

Without the help and support of the above people, Gerald McManis, and my lovely wife, Jackie, this publication would not exist. To all of them, I say thank you.

L. James Harvey, Ph.D.
Director, Education Division
McManis Associates, Inc.

# ABOUT THE AUTHOR

Dr. L. James Harvey is an honors graduate of Hope College in Holland, Michigan. He received his M.A. and Ph.D. degrees from Michigan State University and has served in top administrative positions in both two- and four-year institutions. He has been Dean of Students at Hope College and Dean of Arts and Sciences at the Inter-American University of Puerto Rico. Dr. Harvey has also been Vice President of Student Affairs at William Rainey Harper College in Palatine, Illinois, and President of Prince George's Community College in Maryland.

At Harper College and Prince George's Community College, Dr. Harvey had several years of practical experience in implementing management systems. He is a widely known speaker on the subject and has lectured at colleges and universities from coast to coast. In addition, he has delivered numerous speeches and papers on college management at national conferences and conventions.

Dr. Harvey has assisted many colleges, universities, and governmental agencies in designing and implementing new management systems. He has directed the McManis Associates, Inc. national workshop program which has had hundreds of participants from over 40 states and several foreign countries. His practical experience in implementing management systems is extensive. He currently serves as Director of the Education Division of McManis Associates.

Dr. Harvey is one of the leading exponents of the Management by Objectives (MBO) concept and has authored a popular book on the subject as well as a number of articles on this and other management topics.

## Other Publication by the Author

*Managing Colleges and Universities by Objectives,* Littleton, Colorado: Ireland Education Corporation. 1976 — 106 pp.

iii

## Chapter 1

## INTRODUCTION TO ZERO-BASE BUDGETING

Possibly no period in the history of higher education has contained greater pressures on colleges and universities to be more efficient and effective. Inflation, declining birth rates, the recession, the energy crisis, the movement to clean up the environment, unionism, the student consumer movement, and other factors have all added to the pressures. Calls for greater accountability ring from the rafters of most state legislatures and opinion polls show that the citizens of America have lost a significant amount of faith in the leadership of higher education. Community colleges and school districts are slashing funds for education. School closings and retrenchment plans are major educational occurrences.

All of the above factors and their consequences are causing educators to look at better ways of carrying out the educational enterprise. In many cases, this burden falls on the shoulders of administrators ill-trained to handle the problems. Many educational administrators have not been properly trained to manage large, complex, and changing institutions. Most administrators either have not been educated to be managers or they were prepared in programs long on theory, short on practical applications, and more tuned to the "glory days" of education in the 1950's and 60's, when increasing enrollments and the postwar prosperity made efficiency and effectiveness less necessary. During these decades, educators could make errors and operate "by the seat of their pants" and get away with it. They would just point to the increasing enrollments and use them as evidence that they were doing an outstanding job of offering quality education.

Now the increasing enrollments have stopped and legislators and others are asking embarrassing questions about efficiency and effectiveness. Diminishing resources are requiring some tough decisions. The whole situation is leading to "frayed nerves," rapid turnover in college presidencies, and other unhappy circumstances.

Into the breach have ridden countless authors, consultants, and entrepreneurs with new systems, computerized packages, and quick solution books, workshops, etc. The literature is filled with alphabet soup letters such as Planning, Programming, Budgeting System (PPBS), Management Information System (MIS), Management by Objectives (MBO), and others. While all of these people and systems may have something to contribute, none of them can provide any easy miracle solutions to the problems we face.

The "systems approach" to education, which encompasses the above-mentioned systems, is simply a tool which, if effectively used by competent administrators, can be of help in making the critical decisions that need to be made in our colleges and universities. At best, systems help administrators identify various alternatives and help them select the best course of action from the options open to them. Thus, decision-making is made much easier. Decision-making, by the way, is very easy. The tough part is identifying the various alternatives and gathering the correct data on all the possibilities and options. When this is done effectively, the best alternative is often clearly evident. The systems approach, correctly used, helps to clarify these alternatives and collect the relevant data needed for decision-making.

In the hands of weak or incompoetent administrators, even the best system will fail. Conversely, the best administrators will have some success operating without a system. In the judgement of this author, the college or university that will most effectively (and efficiently) meet the challenges ahead will be the one with a good system used by competent administrators.

Zero-Base Budgeting is a new budgeting approach that focuses on a complete justification of all expenditures each time it is used. Rather than use the previous year's budget as a starting point for the new budget, a "zero-base" is used on the initial assumption.

Zero-Base Budgeting (ZBB) fits into the systems approach and is most effectively used in combination with PPBS and MBO, as will be discussed later. ZBB complements and supplements these other systems and should be used with them, not instead of them.

*Table 1.1* at the end of this chapter attempts to show how these systems fit together in a total systems approach or management system. *Table 1.2* lists some of the benefits that accrue to an institution that uses this approach.

To be effective, each system needs to be carefully "customized" to each institution and fit together with other systems, processes, and procedures. ZBB is no exception.

PPBS came out of the Defense Department back in the early 60's when Robert McNamara was Secretary of Defense. It was a system well-suited to the Department of Defense, but when it was applied to all Federal agencies in 1965, it was less than successful for many reasons — one of which related to the fact that the agencies and situations to which it was applied differed widely. There was little effort to "tailor" or "customize" the system to fit the needs. PPBS has not been greatly successful in higher education for the same reason. Even the very fine efforts of the National Center for Higher Education Management Systems (NCHEMS) in Boulder, Colorado to develop a PPBS for higher education have not been overly successful because there is such great diversity in higher education.

MBO came out of the business world in the 1940's and 50's, and has been tried in higher education over the last 10 years, with mixed results. Failures have occurred as often as successes for a variety of reasons. Two of the most important are the failure to carefully "customize" the system to the college and the lack of expert, fully professional administrators who could understand and use the system.

Now we have ZBB, developed by Peter Phyrr and a team of managers in the late 1960's, and used in the early 1970's at the Texas Instruments Company. Peter Phyrr was then tapped by Governor Jimmy Carter to apply the concept to the State of Georgia in FY 1973. The concept has been little used elsewhere since. However, with Jimmy Carter's election as President and his promise to use ZBB in the Federal Government, the concept is now receiving wide publicity and attention. If carefully used, ZBB can make a valid contribution not only to the Federal Government, but also to higher education because the concept and theory is sound.

What, then, is the concept behind ZBB? The concept is very simple, namely that when developing an organization's budget, it is better not to use the previous year's budget as a base, but rather to start from a zero base (hence, the term Zero-Base Budgeting) and require a justification of all expenditures. Traditionally, budgets have been developed by adding to the previous year's budget. Most organizations would assume that they could add 10% to 15%, or more, to last year's expenditures, and then would set about deciding how the excess would be allocated. Over the years, the validity behind some expenditures ceased to exist, yet the expenditures continued. In some cases, administrators hid money and shifted it around so that they would not lose it. To have one's budget cut, or to fail to get one's "share" of the budget increase was unthinkable for most, and, frequently, was taken as a sign that an administrator was losing his power in the organization. Subordinates often sent their bosses forth to "do battle" for their budget, and his political power and prowess as an administrator were on the line if he did not get what they considered their "fair share." This all led to a tendency to pad or inflate budgets, to factor in these inefficiencies through tradition, and has led to people playing "budget games" rather than focusing on doing a more efficient and effective job.

In short, most organizational budgets contain a good deal of "fat," some of which is locked into the budget through tradition, and the failure to excise vestigal expenditures. Some expenditures which were fully justified in the past may have increased in dollars over the years while the need for them may have diminished or disappeared. With no routine way of dealing with these situations the expenditures just keep on being approved without a thorough review. This ZBB can change.

Probably the single most important reasons for the problems with our traditional budgeting practices in the public sector (colleges, universities, city, state, and Federal agencies) is that there has been no real reward in most organizations for being efficient. As a matter of fact, there has been a penalty attached because if you did not use the money, someone else probably would get it.

It boggles the imagination to think about what would happen if every administrator in charge of a cost center budget in education or government were told that they would get a 20% bonus added to their salaries of any money they could save in the next year's budget without significantly diminishing the effectiveness of their areas. The savings would be unreal, and for once in the months preceding the end of the new budget year, people would not be flying around spending all their budgeted funds for fear that they would lose them next year if they were not expended. I would like to see an organization with the courage to try the above approach, but I would not hold my breath while waiting.

Essentially, then, the human motivation in the budgeting process, in my judgement, has been in the wrong place. Instead of rewarding people for being efficient and effective, the process actually penalizes them. It's only a few, dedicated people who are intrinsically motivated to do a good job, who will actually reduce expenditures when they are not forced to do so by outside forces.

ZBB does not correct the motivational problem automatically, but it does, if properly applied, force each administrator to go back to a zero base and justify each and every expenditure. If used correctly, ZBB throws out the previously stated or implied budget argument that because it was done this way last year, it should be continued. As you will see later on, properly applied, ZBB forces administrators to more conscientiously study alternative methods for providing services and tends to unearth budgetary waste that may have built up over the years.

In the opinion of the author, if ZBB can be combined with a reward system for being efficient, you have the elements for a successful application of ZBB. Without the rewards, the old political budget games will continue, albeit under more stringent rules.

Zero-Base Budgeting is actually more properly called a planning system or a budget planning process. Properly applied, ZBB leads an organization to carefully define, study, and select the best alternatives for each budget period based on the organization's mission, goals, and objectives. It is only after this process is completed that the final budget is put together in the institutional format based on the decisions made in the ZBB process (see Tables 1.1-1.4 at the end of this chapter). This will become clearer to the reader later.

Another point needs to be made regarding the typical budgeting process. Unless an institution has an effective PPBS in place, the budget is frequently developed in isolation from the goals and objectives of the college. Some assumptions are made and judgements rendered about whether planned expenditures are appropriate, but no systematic and routine processes are in place to ensure that the budget and the objectives of the institution are in complete synchronization. An effective PPBS and/or MBO system is an essential adjunct to ZBB, if it is going to be most effectively used.

To say all this in another way, public service organizations need to focus more clearly on their outcomes and what it is they hope to accomplish, set objectives to meet their desired outcomes and then — and only then — select the most efficient and effective means for accomplishing their objectives. It is only after this later step is taken and matched with available resources that a budget can be put together.

Organizations in the private sector have been forced to relate budgets and income more closely to their purposes and outcomes because if they did not, they would go out of business. In the public sector we have often lost sight of our purposes and outcomes because they were not as critical to our income or our budgets as in the private sector. *Table 1.3* is an attempt to illustrate this point. ZBB, properly used in conjunction with other systems, will help public service organizations stay focused on their goals and objectives (purpose) and relate their activities and resources to accomplishing certain clearly defined outcomes.

ZBB can then be defined as a part of the budgeting process which starts from a zero base, disregarding previous years' budgets, and leads to the definition and selection of the most efficient and effective activities and expenditures consistent with meeting the institution's goals and objectives. It should be used with a PPBS or MBO system to have full benefit.

Before proceeding with the next chapter, which will focus on the advantages and disadvantages of ZBB, it is important that selected terms be clarified so that the writer and reader can more effectively communicate. Following are some key definitions used in systems management, ZBB, and this publication.

## BASIC DEFINITIONS

*Cost Center.* A unit or natural grouping of activities in an institution's operations for which costs are collected. These elements or segments are often also budget units for which expenditures are planned.

*Decision Package.* A document which specifies the costs and analysis of an alternative approach to funding a Decision Unit. The key to effective Zero-Base Budgeting is in clearly delineating various decision packages and selecting the best one for each area based on institutional objectives and priorities. There are usually at least three decision packages developed for every Decision Unit.

*Decision Unit.* An element within a budget around which decision packages can be developed. A Decision Unit can be a program, activity, cost center, or sub-unit of a budget which lends itself to ZBB analysis. A list of possible Decision Units for higher education is found in *Appendix A.*

*Goal.* A statement of a single purpose which is a hoped-for accomplishment and derives from the basic mission statement of an institution. A goal is broad, somewhat "motherhoodish," and usually not quantifiable. It is timeless in that it generally has no specific date by which it is to be completed. A goal is a broad statement from which specific objectives can be derived.

*Instruction by Objectives (IBO).* The process of teaching through the use of clearly stated quantifiable behavioral objectives.

*Management Information System (MIS).* An organized method of providing administrators and others in the management process with information needed for decisions, when it is needed, and in a form which aids understanding and stimulates action.

*Management by Objectives (MBO).* A system of managing or administering an organization which places the major focus on fulfilling specific objectives and achieving specified results. In this system, an institution clearly states its main goals and objectives. Program goals and objectives are derived from the institutional process and then each administrator or staff member develops concise, quantifiable objectives which he or she agrees to complete, usually within a twelve-month time frame. The system focuses on planning, directing, and controlling for specified results. MBO differs from other, older management systems in that it stresses objectives and results rather than activities and functions.

*Management by Results.* A synonym for MBO.

*Mission Statement.* A broad, general statement usually no more than a paragraph or two long which sets the parameters for an organization and summarizes the basic purposes for which an institution or program exists.

*Objective.* A clear, concise, specific statement of one intended accomplishment in quantifiable terms. Objectives derive from mission statements and goals and lead to the accomplishment of these elements. An objective may be short-term (one year or less) or long-term (over a year — usually five or ten years). A good objective is quantifiable so that there

can be no question whether or not it has been met within the specified
time period.

*Planning, Programming, Budgeting Evaluation System (PPBES).* The development of a budget by functional programs and the allocation of resources
according to program objectives. Program budgets are usually made on
a one- and five-year basis and should have an evaluation component to
determine whether the program objectives are actually accomplished.
Zero-Base Budgeting supplements PPBES and serves to assist in delineating and selecting alternate approaches to funding the programs. ZBB
really fits into the planning phase of a PPBE System.

*Program.* The composition of all work and related supporting activities undertaken to achieve a *common set* of end objectives.

*Quarterly Review.* In the MBO system, periodic reviews are required by a
manager and his subordinates. At these reviews (usually on a quarterly
basis), objectives are reviewed for progress and validity and an opportunity is provided to delete or modify objectives if changing circumstances so warrant.

*Systems Approach.* A logical, rational procedure for designing a progression
of interrelated components designed to function as a whole in achieving a predetermined objective(s). The methodology includes specifica-
tion of objectives in measurable terms, development of possible approaches, selection of appropriate means to the achievement of the
objectives, integration of approaches into an integrated system, and
evaluation of the effectiveness of the system in attaining the objectives.
MBO and PPBES are examples of systems.

*Zero-Base Budgeting.* A budget planning process based on the assumption
that each expenditure must be justified. Each year, the process starts
with a "zero base," meaning that no past activities or expenditures are
taken for granted. Each activity program or operating unit must justify its existence as well as its request for funds. The process focuses on
establishing decision packages and the selection of the best packages
based on institutional objectives and priorities. *Table 1.4* is one attempt
to illustrate the steps in the ZBB process.

8

## TABLE 1.1

## ACCOUNTABILITY IN HIGHER EDUCATION THROUGH THE SYSTEMS APPROACH

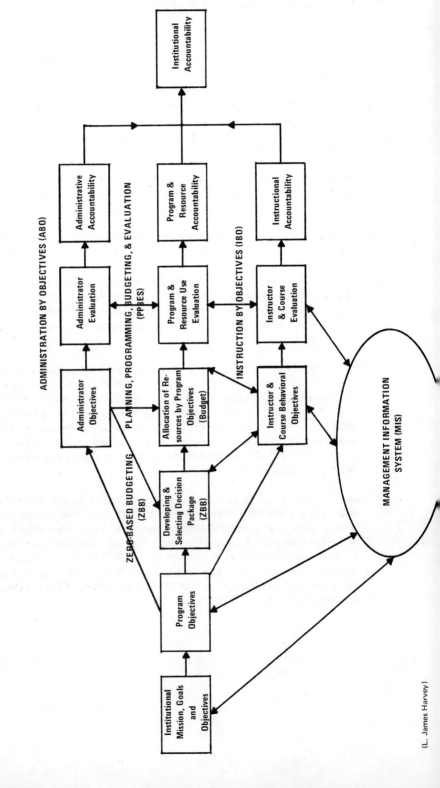

(L. James Harvey)

## TABLE 1.2

## NEEDS MET THROUGH SYSTEMS MANAGEMENT

1. Organizational mission, goals, and objectives are clarified.

2. Programs are related to goals and objectives.

3. The organization focuses on quantifying "outcomes" and evaluation.

*4. Planning is built into the operation of the institution.

*5. Resources are allocated more effectively and priority setting is easier.

*6. Management information is systematically available in an organized and useful format.

7. Administrative effort is effectively focused on institutional goals and objectives. Wasted effort is reduced.

8. Administrators are objectively evaluated.

*9. Information is available for reporting to the board and constituency.

10. Administrators have freedom to operate within clearly defined areas.

*11. Organizational accountability is established.

12. Feedback is available at all levels of the organization.

*13. Communication is facilitated and misunderstandings reduced.

*14. Authority and accountability are delegated to lower levels of the organization in a systematic way.

---

*These are elements where a Zero-Base Budgeting System can make significant contributions.

## TABLE 1.3

## DIFFERENCES IN FUNDING PUBLIC VERSUS PRIVATE SECTORS

### PRIVATE SECTOR
(Business and Industry)

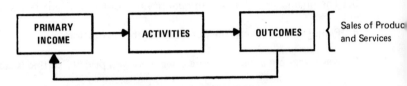

Income and Sale of Outcomes are Directly Related.

### PUBLIC SECTOR

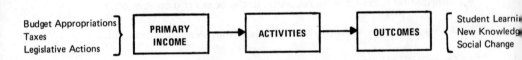

No Direct Relationship Between Outcomes and Primary Income.

*Net Result* is that Public Service Organizations (including Colleges and Universities) often fail to focus on the *quality* of their outcomes and organizational *effectiveness.*

(L. James Harvey)

**TABLE 1.4**

**ZERO-BASED BUDGETING PROCESS**

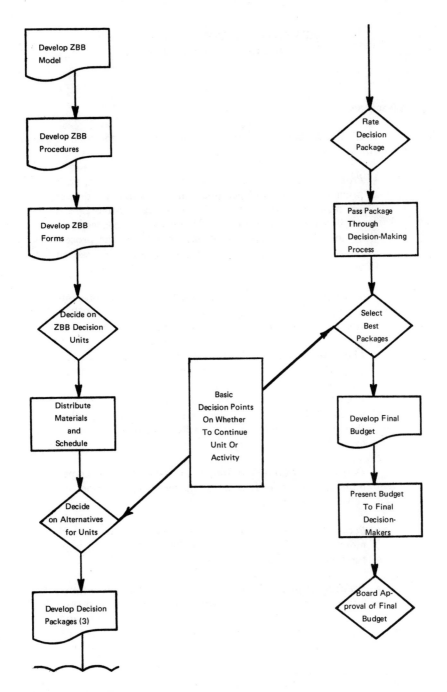

## Chapter 2

# ADVANTAGES AND DISADVANTAGES
# OF ZERO-BASE BUDGETING

## Advantages

If ZBB is properly and effectively implemented, the following advantages should be attained.

- *Produces Annual Program and Expenditure Review.* Each program, activity, or operating unit and all its expenditures are reviewed in depth each year (or however often ZBB is used), and the most efficient and effective approaches to accomplishing the stated objectives are funded. The process replaces the old approach to budgeting which focused on adding (or deleting) a percentage of last year's budget.

- *Tradition Cannot Justify Budget.* An institution prevents history, tradition, or custom from becoming the justification for maintaining certain expenditures.

- *Can Save Money.* An institution can save money by more easily identifying and eliminating vestigal and outdated methods and programs. ZBB also allows for more effective identification of the low cost alternative methods for providing services. A "zero base" is used for planning rather than last year's budget which usually contains programs and expenditures that are outdated.

- *Develops Cost Conscious Staff.* Each staff member becomes more cost conscious, cost-benefit sensitive, and more involved in fiscal planning.

- *Better Staff Morale.* An institution can develop higher staff morale as an open system of budgeting is used with expenditures and programs openly and rationally justified.

- *Reduces Empire Building.* It is extremely difficult for empire building to take place within the processes and procedures of a ZBB system as expenditures undergo open and intense scrutiny every time it is used. Campus politics are also reduced as a factor in determining budget allocations.

- *Easier to Add New Approaches.* The addition of new programs and approaches is more easily accomplished using ZBB, and an institution can more easily adopt to changing conditions. It is easier to add new programs by reducing current costs, allocating new funds, or through minimum funding of the new programs.

- *More Effective Remediation of Staff Weaknesses.* An institution can more easily identify and remediate weak financial planning among the staff. It is strongly urged that each college provide professional development opportunities for the staff, not only to acquaint them with ZBB, but to remediate weaknesses uncovered in the implementing process.

- *Clearer Relation of Budget to Institutional Objectives.* It is easier for an institution to allocate resources in accordance with institutional objectives and priorities.

- *Better Basis for Adjusting to Changing Circumstances.* The list of ranked decision packages can serve as a basis for further planning and budget adjustments that may be required due to changing circumstances.

- *Increases Professional Development.* The whole ZBB process is a professional development activity which should increase the skills and abilities of the institution's managers and make them more effective.

- *Greater Work Satisfaction from Observable Results.* The ZBB system provides concrete feedback from the planning and budgeting process. This, in turn, provides the administrator with a clear indication of how he or she is doing. Positive results give a far greater satisfaction from administrative work than is possible under the traditional budgeting structures.

- *Increases Communication.* As mentioned earlier, there is an increase of communication on significant fiscal issues throughout the organization. This aids morale and leads to greater understanding, which in turn helps to develop a unified effort in achieving the institution's goals and objectives .

- *Better Top Management Decisions.* ZBB gives top management a better view of the total organization from the standpoint of resource allocation, various alternatives possible, and their likely impact on institutional objectives. The process, therefore, allows top management greater flexibility as

they see the various alternatives. They can then more easily
make the broad policy decisions needed to guide the institution.

- *Better Budget Justification.* Institutions will find that budget reviews and approvals by boards, local and state governmental agencies, and constituents will likely be less trouble-
  some if a well thought out ZBB system is used. The review-
  ers are likely to have greater confidence and trust in the
  budget if they know the processes and problems associated
  with ZBB were used.

In addition to the advantages of ZBB, there are also some disadvantages that
may accrue in developing and implementing an effective system.

## Disadvantages

- *Increased Paperwork.* To properly implement ZBB, decision
  packages need to be developed, and an increase in the paperwork associated with this is inevitable. If this is effectively
  done, however, it may reduce some of the typical budget iterations and, therefore, save paperwork from the older budget process. Many colleges and universities go through two
  or three budget iterations before they get a final budget developed in the more traditional approaches. This should be
  reduced to one or two at the most under ZBB.

- *Increased Staff Time.* ZBB, particularly the first time
  through, usually takes longer than the older budget process.
  It can usually be accomplished in a three- to four-month
  period the first time it is used, with average staff time de-
  voted to it. Some additional time is needed to develop the
  process, to educate the staff to the concept, and to implement the processes the first time they are used.

- *Difficulty in Developing and Ranking Decision Units and
  Packages.* It is difficult to define and delineate Decision
  Units and packages and then to rank and select them properly. This is the heart of the process, but it is difficult to do
  effectively.

- *Little Motivation for Staff.* Unless an institution finds some
  way of rewarding the staff who do an effective job in ZBB,
  there will be little motivation for them to function properly

in the system and they will be tempted to play games with it. Most colleges and university budgeting systems actually penalized administrators who save money and increase their efficiency. Generally, the money and staff saved in one area simply is allocated to some other program or area. Unless this type of motivational pattern is changed, it is unlikely that ZBB, or any other budget system, will have any positive or lasting effects.

In summary, there are both advantages and disadvantages associated with using ZBB. The advantages far outweigh the disadvantages and if the proper conditions are present (see Chapter V) in an institution making a successful implementation likely, it should be used. Some of the disadvantages listed above can be reduced or eliminated and some will pertain only in the initial implementing year.

## Chapter 3

## IMPLEMENTING ZERO-BASE BUDGETING

Zero-Base Budgeting is a simple concept to understand, yet it is difficult to implement an effective ZBB system complete with forms, processes, and procedures which accomplishes the intended purposes. It is easy to say that next year's budget will start with a "zero base," and that each and every expenditure must be explained and justified. The distance between stating this and successfully implementing it in a highly complex institution of higher education, most of which are still not united to striving for common objectives, nor oriented to stressing effective management, is considerable.

Following are some recommendations which, if followed, will permit a college or university to maximize their chances of success with ZBB.

1. *Develop an Implementing Plan and Strategy.* Each institution should study its internal situation and then carefully design a timetable for implementing ZBB. *Table 3.1* illustrates a simple Gantt Chart outline of the steps and timetable an institution may wish to follow. Such questions must be answered as: "Will we require ZBB every year, or only once every two to four years?" "Who will quarterback the process and be responsible for it?" "Who will make decisions on which Decision Units will be used?" "Who will be responsible for final decisions on which decision packages will be developed?" "Who will make the final decisions on priorities and selection of final decision packages to go into the final budget?" In other words, a carefully planned systems design effort must be undertaken.

2. *Define and Diagram System.* It is helpful if each system is diagrammed with decision points and time frames clearly laid out, so that everyone will be able to see how the system looks and will function. This process, when laid out, should cover all budget activities, including the final development and approval of the budget.

3. *Design Proper Forms.* Each institution is better off designing forms for decision packages and summary forms (such as for ranking packages) which fit into their current budget and accounting system and fit comfortably into their current systems and terminology.

4. *Educate the Staff.* Each college or university should develop materials and workshops which acquaint the staff with the ZBB concept and the processes, forms, and procedures which will be used by the institution to implement the concept.

5. *Use Expert Help.* The institution should use expert help, particularly in the initial implementation for Items 1, 2, 3, and 4 above. Such help may be available within the university now, or can be secured from consultants outside the institution.

6. *Use the First Time Through as a Trial and "Debugging" Exercise.* The staff should be aware that while you are using ZBB to develop the final budget, nevertheless, the first time through is a trial period after which they will be solicited for comments and suggestions for improving the system.

7. *Provide Resources for Cost Estimating and Data Development.* The heart of a good ZBB system focuses on identifying alternative methods for carrying out activities and then accurately costing out these alternatives. Most staff members will need help and some basic "rules of thumb" to use in costing out new programs. This assistance must be provided and is probably best provided by assigning someone in the business office with this type of expertise to consult with staff members as they develop their decision packages.

8. *Allow Proper Time for Successful Implementation.* The first time through ZBB will take more time. Schedule adequate time so that the staff can implement it in a relaxed, unhurried environment. Depending on the complexity of the institution, how many decision packages you use, and whether you use it throughout the institution or in one area, the time should range from two to four months to complete once the adequate preparations have been made.

There are basically three areas where problems are likely to occur in the ZBB implementing process. The first is in the area of *administrator attitudes.* Doubts, fears, and resistance may develop. Numbers 1 and 4 above are designed to focus on these matters. Unless they are recognized and handled, the system could be seriously damaged before it gets started.

The second area in which problems may develop is in the *decision package formulation.* Problems of which Decision Units to use, how costs are established, and who makes the decisions on which alternatives to use for packages all can cause problems. Elements 1, 2, 3, 4, and 6 above are particularly addressed to these problems.

The third area of problems relates to the *final ranking and decision process.* Who makes the decisions and who has the final voice needs to be clarified. The author firmly believes that ZBB can best function in a framework of participative management where subordinates, while not having a final veto on decisions, do have meaningful and effective input into decisions that affect them and that utilize their expertise.

The implementation of ZBB is a difficult process. All due care needs to be taken if a successful system is to be installed.

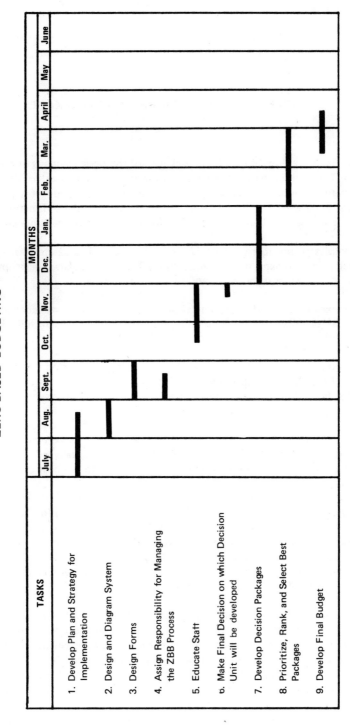

19

**TABLE 3.1**

**SAMPLE SCHEDULE FOR IMPLEMENTING ZERO-BASED BUDGETING***

| TASKS | MONTHS | | | | | | | | | | | |
|---|---|---|---|---|---|---|---|---|---|---|---|---|
| | July | Aug. | Sept. | Oct. | Nov. | Dec. | Jan. | Feb. | Mar. | April | May | June |
| 1. Develop Plan and Strategy for Implementation | | | | | | | | | | | | |
| 2. Design and Diagram System | | | | | | | | | | | | |
| 3. Design Forms | | | | | | | | | | | | |
| 4. Assign Responsibility for Managing the ZBB Process | | | | | | | | | | | | |
| 5. Educate Staff | | | | | | | | | | | | |
| 6. Make Final Decision on which Decision Unit will be developed | | | | | | | | | | | | |
| 7. Develop Decision Packages | | | | | | | | | | | | |
| 8. Prioritize, Rank, and Select Best Packages | | | | | | | | | | | | |
| 9. Develop Final Budget | | | | | | | | | | | | |

* This is a sample based on a first-time application of ZBB and our assumption that the budget for the next fiscal year should be completed and ready for board study and approval by April 1st. Dates can be modified to fit each institution's unique situation.

## Chapter 4

# DEVELOPING DECISION UNITS AND PACKAGES

The Decision Unit and decision package are the basic elements of a ZBB system. The decision package is the basic unit or "building block" of the process. As defined earlier, a Decision Unit is an element within a budget within which decision packages can be developed. It is a program, activity, function, or cost center which has a unity that allows it to be analyzed as a separate entity.

Examples of possible Decision Units in the academic area are: each course, faculty development, departments, "special academic chairs," development of new instructional technology, and summer sessions.

Examples in the student personnel area are: admissions, student records, financial aid, placement, counseling, and residence halls (each individually, if desired).

Examples in the business area are: accounting, purchasing, campus police, trust funds, new construction, and grounds maintenance. Further examples of Decision Units are found in Appendix A.

Decision Units will vary from institution to institution, and may vary within each college or university from year to year. Units may be created to focus attention on various functions. Decision Units are usually subunits of cost centers with two or more commonly aggregating to the cost center budget total.

Institutions will have difficulty in determining which Decision Units to use. If too many are developed, the ZBB system begins to strain under the paperwork, and difficulties arise in effectively prioritizing and analyzing the packages. On the other hand, if too few Decision Units are identified, then the micro-budget analysis is diminished, the chance to uncover savings is reduced, and the ZBB effectiveness is minimized.

For example, a college which has an Office of Admissions and Records which is a separate cost center could conceivably use that office as one Decision Unit. This office would then develop decision packages which encompass all of their activities. On the other hand, within this office, the institution may wish to identify student records, registration, admissions, and student recruitment as separate Decision Units, each of which will develop decision packages.

Using the office as a total unit produces three decision packages, but using the four areas will produce at least twelve. The first approach is easier and less cumbersome, but the latter is more likely to produce a keener analysis of expenditures.

Institutions may wish to vary the number of Decision Units from year to year and even combine the approaches listed above. For example, the Office of Admissions and Records could be a Decision Unit each year except that once every three or four years the four smaller units would be used to produce a more detailed analysis.

The advantage of combining the approaches is that the process is simplified, yet the major benefits of ZBB can still be largely retained. ZBB is most effective the first time it is used; therefore, the above-mentioned alternatives tend to preserve the greatest benefits, while streamlining the process to a certain extent.

Once an institution clarifies and delineates its Decision Units, then it can proceed to develop its decision packages. *Table 4.1* at the end of this chapter illustrates this process. Forms need to be developed such as those found in *Appendix B*. Administrators can then proceed to cost out the various alternatives and packages.

It is desirable for the administrator to work closely with his or her supervisor when developing alternatives and to be mindful of the institutional objectives which hopefully have been previously set and published.

It is also essential at this time to provide assistance to the administrator in costing out the various packages. Someone in the business office should provide consulting help in this area. It is also helpful to provide some "rules of thumb" that can be used to cost out certain aspects of the packages. For example, what percent can be added to salaries to cover fringe benefits, or what average percent will be used to cover salary increases over the years that are projected in the future. With a few key guides such as these, some of which are, in effect, planning assumptions, the administrator can price out his or her packages.

Once the best alternative has been selected for a Decision Unit, the decision package is usually developed in three levels. For most colleges and universities, particularly where administrators cannot be rewarded effectively for outstanding budget work, it is better to ask that packages be developed in three basic areas, such as: minimal, maintenance, and desired. The Los Angeles Community College District uses the designations of skeletal, maintenance, and expansion.

The lowest level should connote a "bare-boned" base operation, below which the existence of the activity would be threatened. Some institutions prefer to state that as a rule, the skeletal level should be a percentage of current year spending (e.g., 75% or 80% of the current year's budget). This has the value of forcing administrators to develop at least one package that is less than current expenditures by a significant amount. Without this provision, some administrators are likely to take the position that the minimum-skeletal level is the current level of spending.

The mid-level, whatever it is called, should be essentially a continuation of present operations or an average level of effort. The upper level should represent an enrichment and an enhancement of the present level of activity and/ or effectiveness. *Table 4.2* illustrates this process further, and uses the designations skeletal, maintenance, and expansion. *Table 4.3* is a further attempt to diagrammatically show how the ZBB process is carried out, focusing particularly on the phases and decision points.

When decision packages have been completed, they are entered into the budget decision-making process. Frequently, this involves the basic administrative structure, as well as budget committees.

It is essential in this process to have institutional objectives and priorities against which to weigh the decisions on accepting or rejecting specific packages. If an effective MBO and PPBS is in place, then it will produce such objectives and priorities; if they are not in place, then the institution should develop a list of priorities for the next year as a bare minimum. Hopefully, administrators would also look into the future (at least five years) to give the decision-makers some direction.

If the administrative organizational structure is used for budget development, then the packages are fed up through the organization. At each level they are reviewed and recommendations sent forward. The ranking and prioritizing of the packages can easily be done on a form similar to that found in *Appendix B. Table 4.4* illustrates how the Decision Units, cost centers, and decision packages might look diagrammatically in an institution.

Most institutions will use a budget committee on some type, even if it is advisory in nature, before the final budget is put together and the president makes final decisions. The decision packages can be presented to the budget committee and actually facilitate its reviewing of the possible expenditures.

# EXAMPLES OF DECISION UNITS AND PACKAGES

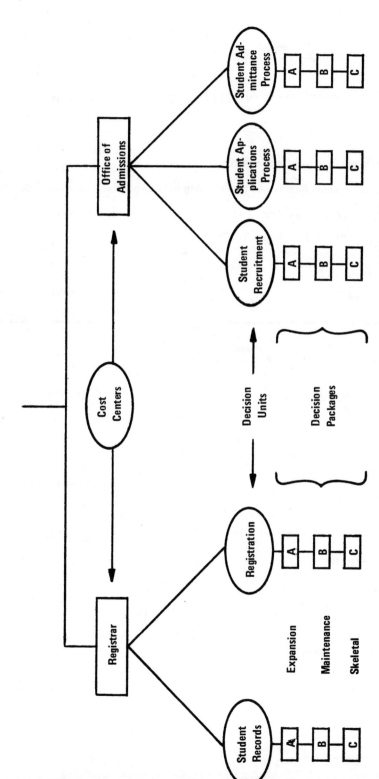

For each Cost Center, a series of one or more Decision Units is established. This is determined by the basic functions or activities within each Cost Center. Following this, alternatives are considered for carrying out each activity or function. When the best activity has been selected, then at least three decision packages are prepared, representing various levels of funding for that activity or function. They are ranked or prioritized and sent through the organizational structure for final decision-making.

24

TABLE 4.2

THREE STEPS IN DEVELOPING DECISION PACKAGES

A.   Clarify and Delineate Decision Unit

B.   Consider Various Alternatives for Providing Activity or Product and Select Best One

C.   Develop at Least Three Decision Packages Covering Various Funding Levels

EXAMPLES

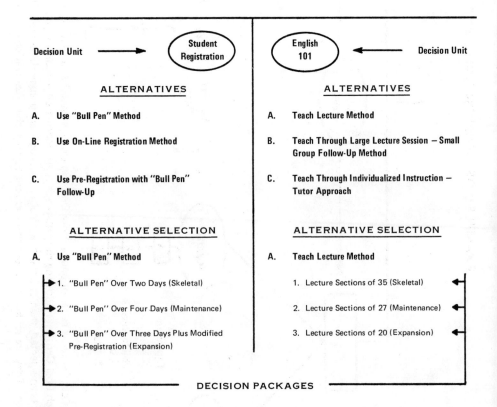

| Decision Unit ⟶ **Student Registration** | **English 101** ⟵ Decision Unit |
|---|---|
| **ALTERNATIVES** | **ALTERNATIVES** |
| A.  Use "Bull Pen" Method | A.  Teach Lecture Method |
| B.  Use On-Line Registration Method | B.  Teach Through Large Lecture Session — Small Group Follow-Up Method |
| C.  Use Pre-Registration with "Bull Pen" Follow-Up | C.  Teach Through Individualized Instruction — Tutor Approach |
| **ALTERNATIVE SELECTION** | **ALTERNATIVE SELECTION** |
| A.  Use "Bull Pen" Method | A.  Teach Lecture Method |
| 1. "Bull Pen" Over Two Days (Skeletal) | 1. Lecture Sections of 35 (Skeletal) |
| 2. "Bull Pen" Over Four Days (Maintenance) | 2. Lecture Sections of 27 (Maintenance) |
| 3. "Bull Pen" Over Three Days Plus Modified Pre-Registration (Expansion) | 3. Lecture Sections of 20 (Expansion) |

DECISION PACKAGES

TABLE 4.3

PHASES AND DECISION POINTS IN ZBB PROCESS

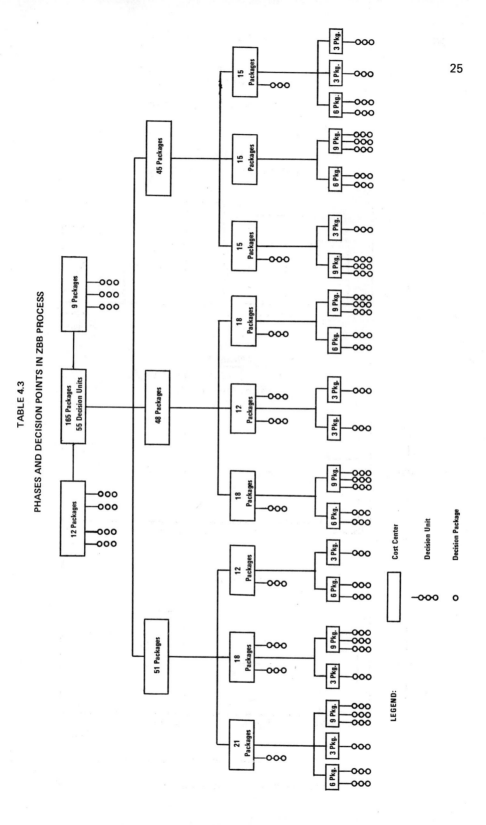

LEGEND:

Cost Center

Decision Unit

Decision Package

## TABLE 4.4

## DECISION POINTS IN ZBB

### PHASE I
### DECISION UNIT ALTERNATIVES[1]

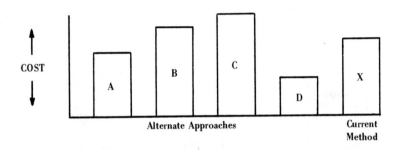

### PHASE II
### DECISION PACKAGE ALTERNATIVES[2]
(If "B" Were Selected)

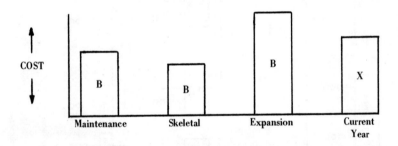

(If "X" Were Selected)

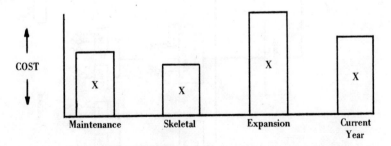

[1] A sixth alternative would be to eliminate the Decision Unit entirely.

[2] At this point, the decision can also be made to eliminate the Decision Unit.

## Chapter 5

## REASONS WHY ZBB FAILS

Zero-Base Budgeting is an easy concept to understand, but as with other new management approaches, it requires great care to effectively implement. There are more reasons why ZBB is likely to fail than there are factors working for its successful implementation.

Below is a list of reasons why ZBB often fails.

1. *Lack of Support from the Top.* Crucial to the implementation is the support and understanding of the top-level administration, particularly the president or chancellor. If he or she does not communicate the importance of the system and if he or she does not link ZBB implementation to whatever reward and punishment system is in effect at the institution, ZBB is likely to fail. As was mentioned earlier, ZBB requires extra work and it may threaten some administrators when they have to produce decision packages that reduce their staffs and expenditures (equated as power by some). Administrators will not be serious about ZBB without some good reason. Top management can provide the motivation and demonstrate, by effective use of ZBB, that it can significantly and positively impact on institutional performance.

2. *Lack of Time to Implement.* As noted in Chapter 3, ZBB requires time to implement. Extra paper work and time to learn the system are required. An institution that is not ready to devote the time necessary is apt to fail with ZBB, or, at best, to achieve only a superficial implementation which contains few real benefits.

3. *The Assumption that Current Methods are Optimal and Cannot be Improved.* Strangely enough, in spite of all evidence to the contrary, some educators believe that the way they are currently doing things is nearly perfect and cannot be improved. This attitude will kill any attempts to improve and add new systems, including ZBB.

4. *Attempts to Implement ZBB Overnight.* ZBB requires time, effort, and extensive preparation if it is to succeed. The Time-Phased Plan of Action in Chapter 3, which lays out an eight- to nine-month implementation plan, is about as fast as this process can be carried out. To attempt to "crash" the installation of a system can significantly handicap any implementation. If negative attitudes are present in the administrative staff that must be overcome first, then the process may take even

longer to implement. One caution — go slowly and do not try to force
the system too fast. Administrators who oppose it strongly can play
games with it and strip it of much of its value. They can do this by failing to do effective work in developing the decision packages.

5.    *A Paper Mill is Created.* Keep the forms and procedures simple. If exotic
      "bells and whistles" are added to the system in the design of forms and
      processes, the system may become so cumbersome that it becomes an
      end in itself. Administrators may also spend so much time reading man-
      uals and trying to understand the system that they lose sight of their
      main tasks. Elaborate forms asking for great details on plans for carry-
      ing out various alternatives and decision package elements will probably
      help kill an effective ZBB implementation. This may cause ZBB to be-
      come an end in itself rather than a means to an end. If this is done, then
      ZBB itself will become a major problem, and perhaps a "scapegoat" for
      continued poor management.

6.    *Omission of an Educational Component.* It is essential that the staff be
      educated fully in the theory and rationale for ZBB, as well as in the pro-
      cesses and procedures to be used in each institution. If hostile attitudes
      and resistance are present, they need to be neutralized before the im-
      plementation goes forward. Staff development workshops, seminars,
      readings, and tutorials may be used to assist in the educational process.

7.    *Lack of Cost Estimation Assistance and Individual Assistance.* Many ad-
      ministrators will need help in developing their decision packages and in
      following the ZBB processes, particularly the first time through. Some-
      one should be trained and prepared to provide this assistance. If it is
      not easily available, then frustrations will build up. The system will suf-
      fer from a lowered staff morale and effort.

8.    *Lack of Clear Decision-Making Structure.* It should be crystal clear as to
      how the decision packages and alternatives will be handled in the insti-
      tutional decision-making processes. The decision process should be dia-
      grammed and clear. If the staff does not know who is making these de-
      cisions, or what the process is, they will likely lose confidence in the
      system and play games with their submission of material. The staff par-
      ticularly needs to know how they fit into the process and what impact
      their recommendations will be likely to have.

9.    *Failure to Reward Those Who Increase Efficiency.* The whole matter of
      motivation is critical. This issue was touched upon in Chapter 1 and will
      be dealt with again in the next chapter. Without rewarding administra-
      tors or faculty who save money and who find more efficient ways of

performing their activities, there is no real motivation for using ZBB effectively. As a matter of fact, using ZBB without an effective motivational structure will simply perpetuate "playing games" with the whole budget process. Most current rewards go to those who get more staff and money in their budgets. Rewards should go to those who are the most efficient and effective.

10. *Implementation is Attempted in an Unhealthy Environment.* If an institution has low morale among the staff and/or if major internal problems exist, do not try to implement ZBB. Deal with the "health" problems of the institution first. If ZBB implementation is attempted in an unhealthy environment, it will simply get caught in the "cross-fire" and fail. It is also unwise to implement the system if an institution is without a full-time or permanent president. Wait until the new person is in place and then go forward, but only if this is something that the new chief executive wants, will use, and will support with the full force of the top office.

11. *Using ZBB in a Highly Political Environment.* If an institution is highly political, meaning that major decisions are made more on the basis of power, self-interests, and political forces inside and outside the institution, then forget ZBB. ZBB is a management tool for use by professional managers who are basically motivated by working together in a team relationship to improve institutional performance. If the institutional decision-making processes are significantly impacted by arbitrary judgements rendered by self-serving political elements, ZBB will, at best, be a time wasting exercise in futility, which will diminish staff morale as they see political judgements supercede correct professional decisions.

12. *Failing to Link ZBB to Institutional Objectives and Priorities.* ZBB provides a multitude of variables and alternatives for decision-making. Unless there is a clear framework of objectives and priorities in the institution from which to work in selecting the best decision packages, the process is likely to produce more frustration than help. A good PPB or MBO system is essential if ZBB is to work. Alternately, institutional goals and objectives can be linked to the ZBB system as an extension of the system.

## Chapter 6

## PEOPLE PROBLEMS AND OPPORTUNITIES

Zero-Base Budgeting must impact on the total budget. Since the largest expenditures for most organizations relate to people and their salaries, this area needs special attention. The question was recently raised as to whether ZBB should affect personnel. The questioner's institution expended 85% of its budget on salaries. If ZBB did not impact on personnel, the total effects of its use would be limited to 15 to 20% of most college and university budgets which are non-personnel related. This would seriously limit the value of ZBB and, in truth, prevent ZBB from being "zero-based."

It is also axiomatic that the most difficult parts of a budget to deal with are those that relate to people and staffing. In most cases, colleges and universities would not just fire people (even if they could) if programs or activities were eliminated. How, then, can ZBB be of any value where 60-95% of the budget includes people and their salaries, fringe benefits, and so forth?

The response to the above question is that the larger the percentage of the budget is salaries, the more difficult it is — but it is not impossible. The remainder of this chapter attempts to analyze this matter and give some suggestions regarding the people problems and opportunities.

Essentially, there are four basic ways in which administrators, faculty, staff, and classified employees can be dealt with if, through the ZBB (or other system), the institution decides to eliminate a program or activity. First, a person can be terminated or released outright. Second, they can be transferred to another area where there is an opening or where they can be more effectively utilized. Third, they may leave or be encouraged to resign in order to accept a more attractive employment opportunity outside the institution. The fourth and last way is that the institution may encourage or promote early retirements which may be in the best interests of the person and the institution.

In addition to these four areas over which the college or university has some control, there is some natural attrition in institutions because of resignations, deaths, pregnancies, or other factors leaving personnel openings, which can, in some cases, be used to provide the institution with the flexibility to adjust to needed personnel reductions.

Each of the above need some further discussion.

1.  *Terminations.* Most institutions will obviously hesitate to use this method except as a last resort. Humanistic concerns, possible lawsuits, tenure policies, union contracts, and other factors make this one of the least-used methods of reducing personnel. It is most often used when financial conditions so deteriorate that retrenchment is essential to institutional survival. In most cases, an institution has the right to terminate employees if a program or activity is eliminated; however, the right is not often used.

    This method is more humane if the institution goes out of its way to find the terminated employees new positions, and even share in relocation costs if a change of areas is necessary. An institution may decide to pay fees for employment services and use their offices to relocate terminated staff, thus reducing some of the negative factors involved in termination. These actions, plus proper advanced notice to employees (usually three to six months, at a minimum), can take some of the "sting" out of the termination process. Termination leaves, with part of total pay for a short period; termination pay; and other devices may also relieve some of the problems. In short, the termination process can be used, though it is difficult at best. However, through the use of various devices, the process can be more humane and less traumatic.

    The above statements apply to terminations made because of program changes. Some institutions will occasionally terminate employees for incompetence or other reasons related to just causes. While these terminations seldom, if ever, correlate with program modifications, when they occur they should be reviewed to see if they may provide the opportunity for the institution to deal more effectively with its personnel strategies, particularly in relation to Number 2, below. The terminations of this nature may also trigger the institution's review of the program through the ZBB methodology in order to possibly take advantage of the personnel vacancy.

    In addition to the above, institutions may wish to counsel terminated employees and even retrain some employees for jobs outside the institution. More will be said about this in the next section.

2.  *Transfers.* Employees can be transferred to other areas within the institution if the activity they are a part of is eliminated or reduced in scope. This may be difficult and could involve morale problems if the transfer is to an area the employee dislikes or if it is to a lower-level position (perceived or real). On the other hand, a transfer may stimulate an employee with a new challenge and it could even be perceived as an upward move. If the transfer were to a new, highly visible activity, it could be personally and professionally very attractive. This process is more likely to be viable in a large institution. It does not reduce staff, but it does allow more effective use of staff and could lead to eliminating other costs associated with a discontinued activity.

It seems logical that colleges and universities could make themselves more flexible if they would become more involved in educating and upgrading their employees. Professional development programs which broaden employees, make them more versatile, and add skills, also provide the institution with flexibility in moving employees and in adapting to change.

For example, a student financial aid counselor who, through broadening experiences and further education, develops skills as a counselor or student activities aide, not only expands his or her horizons and makes promotion more likely, but, if the financial aid program is suddenly reduced, there are other areas of the college to which he or she can be assigned permanently or temporarily while seeking other employment.

Educators are notorious for promoting more education for everyone but themselves. Most colleges have very little money for in-service and professional development activities. Not only is this type of education essential for staying relevant in this time of rapid change, but it also provides the institution with the type of flexibility mentioned above.

It might also be noted that a good professional development program might make employees more susceptible to promotional opportunities outside the institution. This is true, but it is not all bad. A reasonable turnover of employees is good in the sense that it allows new blood and new ideas to come into an institution. It is only when excessive turnover due to management problems, low pay, or other factors that might seriously and negatively affect operations occur that this is detrimental.

In summary, then, transferring people inside an institution can be accomplished when activities are reduced or eliminated and, if carefully planned, it could be done to the benefit of both the employee and the institution.

3.    *Resignations.* There are some ways in which an institution can promote timely resignations. An employee might be promised some special training and help in relocating in another area or profession. Peter Drucker, the eminent management consultant, has recently recommended that higher education seriously consider retraining some of the non-productive and mediocre scholars in our institutions so that they can get into more productive positions in other professions. His suggestion provides opportunities in a tight job market for employment of younger scholars who would infuse our institutions with new blood and fresh ideas.

The same process recommended by Peter Drucker could be used to encourage faculty or administrators in activities that are being eliminated to leave the institution for a new, and, hopefully, more challenging professional position. If this process is coupled with employment assistance, it might encourage some productive mid-career shifts that could be exciting for staff members. A large college or university might give free tuition or other benefits to encourage staff to train further and leave.

Cash bonuses or loans to stimulate a staff member to go into business might be considered to encourage a timely resignation if this is legal and attractive to the individual.

Terminal sabbatical leaves at full or part salary might also be offered. These could be attractive to some staff, particularly if they want to re-tool, regroup, and change positions.

4.    *Early Retirements.* Most of the inducements above can also be used in one form or another to encourage early retirements. Some staff members would be delighted to leave early for a variety of reasons, particularly if they have something to gain. If early retirement reduces benefits, the difference might be made up by the institution or by the promise of part-time teaching or other assignments.

In addition to the four basic ways in which our institutions can shift or part company with employees, the institution can also take advantage of natural attrition among the staff.   This attrition can run as high as 15 to 20% in some organizations (even higher if serious internal problems exist). Resignations, deaths, retirements, pregnancies, and other factors would cause some attrition in the staff. An institution can use these circumstances to review (if they do not do so every year) the activity or program with ZBB procedures. If they find that a reduction or elimination of the program is desirable, they will have less personnel problem to deal with.

As a matter of fact, it is not a bad idea for every institution to review formally, as a matter of policy, every position that becomes vacant to ensure that before it is refilled, it is indeed needed and not just a vestige of the past.

There are many ways to deal effectively and creatively with the people problems. I am sure that the reader and others can come up with other suggestions. As a matter of fact, many of the solutions can be both to the benefit of the employee as well as the institution.

One additional and important point needs to be made. The institution that looks ahead three to five years and plans carefully is in a much better position to deal with people problems and opportunities. Retirements can be anticipated, program reviews scheduled to coincide with natural vacancies, programs phased in or out, retraining and transfers planned carefully, and so forth. The institution that tries to deal with this on a year-to-year basis has a much more difficult time. Used most effectively, ZBB asks for projections of at least three years and may well coincide with the more commonly used five-year cycle.

In summary, the fact that most institutions have budgets that are heavily weighted with salaries should not eliminate the possibility of effectively using ZBB. It can, in effect, be used and the people problems can, with effort, even become opportunities to assist staff members to accomplish new objectives.

## Chapter 7

## SELECTED COMMENTS ON ZBB

Following are some selected comments about ZBB which will help the reader clarify some of the issues regarding ZBB.

*ZBB is a planning and budget development system rather than the budget itself.* A ZBB system, properly implemented, encompasses the planning that should go into the processes that precede the development of a final budget. It is a planning process in the sense that, if properly used, the institution studies, in a methodical way, the various alternatives open to it in accomplishing its objectives, as well as the many options available for funding needed activities. As was noted earlier, the ZBB process must be linked to clearly stated institutional objectives and priorities, or there is great risk that once the alternative methods and decision packages have been developed, the final decisions will be made arbitrarily and without regard to institutional direction. If the latter is going to be the case, an institution need not bother going through the ZBB process. It would just be cosmetic.

*Motivation is the key.* This matter was touched on in Chapter 1, but should be expanded upon here. The typical pressures and motivations in institutional budget development and expenditures are just the opposite of what they should be. Because we generally equate large staffs and expenditures with power and status, it is a truism that an administrator who can increase his or her staff and budget gains in these factors. Empire building is a common phenomenon present in varying degrees in most institutions.

C. Northcote Parkinson, in his book, *Parkinson's Law, and Other Studies in Administration,* * reveals that staff members will increase 5.75% per year in organizations, regardless of whether there is more or less work to do. Parkinson says this fact is based on two axioms: (1) An official wants to multiply subordinates, not rivals; and (2) Officials make work for each other. In short, there is automatic upward pressure on budgets, regardless of work load; new, more efficient technology; better ways of doing things, etc. Officials propose new subordinates because this means more influence and power. It may also mean less work for them. These are the basic factors in empire building and budgetary inflation.

---

*Parkinson, C. Northcote, *Parkinson's Law and Other Studies in Administration*. Ballantine Books, New York, 1964.

If the motivation is all pushing in the direction of larger staffs and budgets, how can ZBB be effective? To be concise, in that instance, ZBB cannot help much. ZBB can, however, make it more difficult for administrators to hide surplus funds and unnecessary staff, and it can make the game tougher for the empire builders to play, but that's about it.

In the judgement of this writer, the only answer to efficiency in education and government is to change the motivational direction. Aside from the few self-actualized, intrinsically motivated administrators who get their primary motivation from doing a job well, most administrators are impacted strongly by the external motivational factors noted earlier. The only way to effectively involve them in the budget process is to reward them for saving money and operating efficiently.

This can be done, but attitudes must change in public service organizations. Rewards must be given. Whether these rewards are bonuses, salary increases, professional development opportunities, vacations, trophies, promotions, public recognition, or other forms, they will have to outweigh the rewards of a larger empire, or the system will never work.

Recalling the earlier example, can you imagine what would happen if all the administrators in education and government were told that they could keep in the form of a bonus 20% of all the money they could save in next year's budget without reducing program effectiveness? I do not believe our national economy could stand the shock that the change would bring.

To put it plainly, if a college or university is ever going to harness all of its brain power to focus on efficiency in operation, then either the institution must hire an entire staff of self-actualized, highly motivated, intrinsically driven, altruistic professionals, or they must find a way to reward the staff for efficient operations above and beyond the natural motivation to build power bases and empires.

It can be done, but it seldom has. Without the above, ZBB and a good administrative evaluation system can only take an institution so far. Maybe it is all that can be done. I do not believe so, but even the ZBB-Devaluation system are well worth attempting.

*Eliminating people is a problem.* Some people say that ZBB will not work very well in institutions of higher education because most of the budget is in salaries, and with tenure, unions, court suits, and so forth, reducing staffs is impossible. Since 70-90% of most budgets are people, they do have a point; however, a couple of other points need to be made.

First, ZBB focuses on the addition of new programs and staff, as well as current elements. A good ZBB system will help to prevent unnecessary additions and should slow the application of Parkinson's Law, if not eliminate its impact altogether.

Secondly, there are mechanisms for staff reduction that can be used. Retrenchment is an often-used word today, and it can be used — tenure and unions notwithstanding. Aside from retrenchment which does, after proper procedures are followed, allow dismissal of an employee, an institution can also take advantage of early retirements, resignations, transfers, and other opportunities provided by natural staff "attrition." If an institution is effectively using ZBB, then it is in a far better position to take optimum advantage of chances to shift, reduce, or restructure personnel.

In short, the fact that college and university budgets are largely made up of salaries and people may be more an argument for, rather than against, using ZBB. The people problem can be more effectively analyzed and integrated into the resource allocation process with ZBB than without it. Chapter 6 expands on this point of how to effectively handle the people problems and opportunities in a ZBB system.

*Should ZBB be used every year?* There are valid arguments, pro and con, in this regard. The arguments for using ZBB every year are:

1. *Different budget processes would be needed for "off years."*

2. *If circumstances change, there is no capability for modifying the budget without ZBB and the alternatives it presents.*

3. *Administrators may go back to "bad habits" in between years when ZBB is used.*

4. *There is a chance for Parkinson's Law to apply in off years.*

5. *Programs that should be eliminated will continue without review.*

6. *Administrators get better at it and improve their use of the system if it is used every year.*

Arguments for not using ZBB every year are:

1. *The greatest benefits accrue the first time ZBB is used and diminish somewhat thereafter. Using ZBB every three or four years may bring the same benefits as using it every year.*

2. *The process is time-consuming.*

3. *There may be a tendency to get the same package every year.*

4. *Programs can be reviewed each year even without ZBB.*

5. *Programs and activities do not change much from year to year, and an occasional ZBB review is sufficient.*

Each institution will have to weight the above factors for itself and make its own decision. The basic options are as follows:

*1. Use ZBB every year.*

*2. Use ZBB every three or four years.*

*3. Use ZBB in a revolving manner so that some part (Instruction, Student Personnel, Business, or subdivisions of these) of the institution is using it each year and each area must use it once every three or four years.*

*4. Use ZBB every three to four years, but require its use in between times in areas where new programs or activities are proposed or in Decision Units where special attention is desired for some reason.*

**The *"sunset concept" and ZBB*.** One of the concepts that is gaining in popularity in government and one which has some relevance for education is the "sunset concept." Basically, this concept or principle is that any program or activity should only be approved for a fixed period of, say, three to five years. After this period, it is assumed that the program will self-destruct, unless its extension can be fully justified. In short, the program would have to go through the same kind of justification review and analysis that it did when it was first proposed. Of course, there would be the additional component of the careful analysis of what the program had accomplished since its inception.

In short, all activities, programs, cost centers, or Decision Units would have the "sunset" on them, and a thorough review would occur. Unless this review dictated continuation, the program would automatically cease to exist or be replaced by one of significantly different make-up, which might better accomplish the original program objectives.

This "sunset" principle could be coupled with the processes and procedures of ZBB, as well as those of Program Audits (see following section). ZBB principles, used at the end of the approval period (sunset) would provide for a thorough review of the alternatives to meeting the objectives of the program. All college or university programs could be put on a three to four year approval basis so that a portion of them would be under intensive scrutiny each year.

**Program Audits and ZBB.** A growing trend in higher education is to have each program, activity, or Decision Unit undergo a Program Performance Audit every four or five years. These audits are usually conducted by persons outside the institution who are experts in the area under review. These reviews focus on efficiency and effectiveness and help the institution in evaluating itself.

Program Audits could easily and effectively be combined with the "sunset" principle and ZBB to give an institution a powerful force for keeping itself relevant, efficient, and effective.

Program Audits could be timed to occur at the beginning of the last year before the "sunset" on the program. The audit could help determine: the relevance of the program; whether it should be continued; and, if continued, whether it should be significantly modified. The audit could provide alternatives and input into the ZBB process if it were used in conjunction with the audit. The new budget for the program, if it were to continue, could be in the ZBB framework.

The Program Audit, the "sunset" principle, and ZBB give an institution powerful accountability tools. Any board or public critics would be hard-pressed to fault an institution that was effectively using these tools. The relevance, efficiency, and effectiveness of every program would be under routine scrutiny and analysis, including objective analysis if the Program Audit is used.

## Chapter 8

## SUMMARY AND CONCLUSIONS

ZBB is likely to be a buzz word in the years to come, as were Planning, Programming, Budgeting System (PPBS) and Management by Objectives (MBO) before it. Having used ZBB in Georgia, President Jimmy Carter will popularize the concept as he attempts to apply it at the Federal Government level.

If ZBB follows PPBS and MBO, it will be a failure as a system, but a success as a concept and a positive residue of thought and action will be left behind. PPBS came out of the Defense Department and was forced on the Federal bureaucracy. As a system, it did not succeed, but a residual of program planning and evaluation took hold and still remains from this attempt to implement the system.

More recently, MBO met the same fate. President Nixon's corporate advisors brought this concept to Washington and tried to use it to manage. The Federal bureaucracy "spit it up," as it had PPBS before it, but, again, a residue of objectives setting and measurements of accomplishments, as well as pockets of full blown use of MBO remain.

The chances are that ZBB will not succeed as a system. At least the odds are strongly against it. However, it is equally as likely that the concept of frequent, perhaps annual, program review, alternate costing, and the routine linking of cost benefits to broad objectives will remain and serve the government well.

Those in institutions of higher education would do well to review the ZBB concept and to use it as appropriate. As has been indicated, there are a wide variety of options for using ZBB, as there are with PPBS and MBO.

Educators must, if efficiency and effectiveness are to be cherished, sort out the unique ways in which they can weld the principles of these systems, including ZBB, into an effective management system. Each institution must develop its system around its uniquenesses and should be hesitant to borrow a "package" that someone else is using or is selling. The design of a unique system is an existing management challenge for this generation of administrators.

Peter Drucker has said that the greatest challenge in management in this century is to manage public service organizations for *effectiveness.* He also said that the greatest need we have is for a management system. PPBS, MBO, and ZBB offer elements of a management process that should be carefully studied and analyzed for the contributions they can make to our day-to-day operational systems.

This publication has attempted to give the reader a brief, concise overview of one of these systems — Zero-Base Budgeting. It has endeavored to acquaint the reader with the concept, its application, its advantages and its shortcomings, and to show how it can be implemented. This was done in the hope that the reader will be able to separate fact from fiction and utilize the concept effectively if it is appropriate to the reader's situation.

# APPENDIX A

## CHECKLIST OF POSSIBLE DECISION UNITS

## CHECKLIST OF POSSIBLE DECISION UNITS

### INSTRUCTION

Divisions or Departments (Each Separately)
Courses (By Course or Similar Course Grouping)
Academic Administration
Instructional Support
"Special Academic Chairs"
Computer-Assisted Instruction
Faculty Development
Development of New Instructional Techniques
Continuing Education
Summer Session
Overseas Programs
Remedial or Developmental Education
Sabatical Leaves
Off Campus Centers (By Center)

### LEARNING RESOURCE CENTER

Administration
Cataloging
Photocopy and Microfilm
New Book Purchases
Subscriptions
General Service (Checkout, Reference, etc.)
Book Binding

### STUDENT SERVICES

Admissions
Student Records
Registration
Financial Aid
Student Activities
Lecture-Concert Series
Counseling
Placement
Residence Halls
Intramurals
Intercollegiate Athletics
College Union
Testing and Evaluation
Health Services
Graduate Admissions
Student Orientation
Student Judicial Affairs
Student Recruitment

### ADMINISTRATION

Office of the President
Executive Management
University Relations
Alumni Relations
College Information Services
Computer Services
Institutional Research
Legal Services
Professional Development
Board of Trustees
Endownment Management
Planning Coordination
Program Evaluation

### BUSINESS AFFAIRS

Accounting
Purchasing
Building Maintenance
Grounds Maintenance
New Construction
Campus Police
Campus Fire Department
Trust Funds
Preventative Maintenance (Equipment)
Auxiliary Services (By Separate Service)
Personnel
Facilities Planning and Development
Cash Flow Management
Payroll
Controller's Office
Annual Audit
Fringe Benefits

**APPENDIX B**

**SAMPLE FORMS FOR DECISION PACKAGES**

# ZBB FORM 1
## DECISION PACKAGE

| 1. Decision Unit | 2. Person Preparing | 3. Priority Rating | 4. Cost Center |
|---|---|---|---|

| 5. Package | | 6. Date Prepared | 7. No. of Similar Packages | 8. Total Cost | |
|---|---|---|---|---|---|
| Number | Level | | | Last Year | This Package |

**9. Objectives of this Package; Code to Higher Objectives** (Use Other Side, If Necessary, for Items 9, 10, and 11)

**10. Advantages/Disadvantages Over Other Packages**

**11. Key Differences from Other Packages**

| 12. Cost Factors | | This Year's Cost For Function | Estimated Costs | | | % Year 1 Over Last Year | |
|---|---|---|---|---|---|---|---|
| Acct. No. | Function | | Year 1 | Year 2 | Year 3 | Increase | Decrease |
| | Professional Staff (No.) | | | | | | |
| | Support Staff (No.) | | | | | | |
| | Supplies | | | | | | |
| | Equipment | | | | | | |
| | Travel | | | | | | |
| | Contractual Services | | | | | | |
| | Miscellaneous | | | | | | |
| | TOTAL | | | | | | |

APPENDIX B

## ZBB FORM 2
## DECISION PACKAGE SUMMARY FORM

| Program Area: | | | Prepared By: | | | | |
|---|---|---|---|---|---|---|---|
| Acct. No. | Rank of Package | Title of Decision Package | This Yr.'s Budgeted Costs | 1st Year | 2nd Year | 3rd Year | % Increase/ Decrease Over this Year |
| | | | | | | | |

**APPENDIX C**

**BIBLIOGRAPHY OF READINGS ON
ZERO-BASE BUDGETING**

## BIBLIOGRAPHY OF READINGS ON
## ZERO-BASE BUDGETING

The following are some books, articles, and miscellaneous publications relative to ZBB. Since the concept is new, few comprehensive materials have yet been published on the subject. Peter Phyrr's book (listed below) is probably the best single source material on the subject at this time. Other books listed below cover ZBB in sections or chapters and focus on related materials.

### BOOKS

Cheek, Logan M., *Zero-Base Budgeting Comes of Age.* New York: American Management Assoc., 1977.

Georgia, Office of Planning and Budget. *General Budget Preparation Procedures, Fiscal Year 1978 Budget Development.* Atlanta: 1976, (31p.).

Hogan, Roy L. *Zero-Base Budgeting: A Rationalistic Attempt to Improve the Texas Budget System.* Austin: University of Texas, 1975, (152 p.).

Lee, Robert D., Jr., and Ronald W. Johnson. *Public Budgeting Systems.* Baltimore: University Park Press, 1973.

Merewitz, Leonard, and Stephen Sosnick. *The Budget's New Clothes: A Critique of Planning, Programming, Budgeting and Benefit-Cost Analysis.* Chicago: Markham Publishing Co., 1971, (318 p.).

Minmier, George S. *An Evaluation of the Zero-Base Budgeting System in Governmental Institutions.* Atlanta: Georgia State University, School of Business Administration; Research Monograph No. 68, 1975, (264 p.).

Pyhrr, Peter A. *Zero-Base Budgeting: A Practical Management Tool for Evaluating Expenses.* New York: Wiley, 1973, (231 p.).

Schultze, Charles L. *Politics and Economics of Public Spending.* Washington, D.C.: Brookings Institute; H. Rowan Gaither, Lectures in Systems Science, 1968, (143 p.).

Wildavsky, Aaron. *Budgeting: A Comparative Theory of the Budgetary Process.* Boston: Little, Brown, Inc., 1975, (432 p.).


## PERIODICALS


Axelrod, Donald. *The State of the Art or Science of Budgeting, Public Administration Review,* Vol. 33 (November-December, 1973), 576-584.

Broder, David S. *A Closer Look at Zero-Base Budgeting, The Washington Post,* August 8, 1976, p. C-8.

Brueningsen, Arthur F. *SCAT — A Process of Alternatives, Management Accounting,* (November 1976), 56-60, 66.

*Can Congress Control the Bureaucracy?, Association Management,* (August 1976), 55-57.

Granof, Michael H., and Dale A. Kinzel. *Zero-Based Budgeting: A Modest Proposal for Reform, The Federal Accountant,* Vol. 23 (December 1974), 50-56.

Havemann, Joel. *Congress Tries to Break New Ground, The National Journal,* Vol. 8 (May 22, 1976), 706-713.

LaFaver, John D. *Zero-Base Budgeting in New Mexico, State Government,* Vol. 47 (Spring 1974), 108-112.

Martz, Larry. *Say-Nay Politics, Newsweek,* (June 7, 1975).

McGinnis, James F. *Pluses and Minuses of Zero-Base Budgeting, Administrative Management,* Vol. 37 (September 1976), 22-23+.

Minmier, George S., and Roger H. Hermanson. *A Look at Zero-Base Budgeting — The Georgia Experience, Atlanta Economic Review,* Vol. 26 (July-August, 1976), 5-12.

Murray, Thomas J. *The Tough Job of Zero Budgeting, Dun's Review,* Vol. 104 (October 1974,) 70-72+.

National Governors' Conference. *Innovations in State Government: Messages from the Governors,* "Planning a Budget from Zero," Jimmy Carter, p. 41-48. Reprinted in *The Congressional Record,* Vol. 122 (February 25, 1976), p. H1314-H1315.

Peirce, Neil R. *State-Local Report — Structural Reform of Bureaucracy Grows Rapidly, National Journal Reports.* (April 5, 1975).

Pyhrr, Peter A. *Zero-Base Budgeting, Harvard Business Review*, Vol. 48 (November-December, 1970), 111-121.

Pyhrr, Peter A. *Zero-Base Budgeting: Where to Use It and How to Begin, S.A.M. Advanced Management Journal*, Vol. 41 (Summer 1976), 4-14.

Singleton, David W., and others. *Zero-Based Budgeting in Wilmington, Delaware, Government Finance*, Vol. 5 (August 1976), 20-29.

Stonich, Paul J. *Zero-Base Planning — A Management Tool, Managerial Planning*, (July-August, 1976), 1-4.

*Toughness by the Numbers, Forbes*, (September 1, 1976), 26-27.

*Ways to Make Uncle Sam Spend More Wisely, Nation's Business*, Vol. 60 (August 1972), 26-28.

Wildavsky, Aaron, and Arthur Hammann. *Comprehensive versus Incremental Budgeting in the Department of Agriculture, Administrative Science Quarterly*, Vol. 10 (December 1965), 321-346.

*Zero-Base Budgeting — An Exercise in Decision-Making, U.S. General Accounting Office*, (August 1976).

*Zero-Base Budgeting: One Way to Erase Needless Government Programs, Nation's Business*, (November 1976), 52-54, 56.

## MISCELLANEOUS MATERIALS

Leininger, David L., and Ronald C. Wong. *Zero-Base Budgeting in Garland, Texas.* A report prepared by MAC with a member of the Garland city staff.

State of Georgia. *General Budget Procedures and Instructions, Fiscal Year 1977 Budget Development.*

State of Illinois, Department of Personnel. *Fiscal Year 1977 Budget Preparation Instructions and Examples of Submissions.*

State of New Jersey, Department of the Treasury, Budget Bureau. *Manual for Preparation of Budget Requests (April 1974).*

State of Texas, Legislative Budget Board. *Fiscal Year 1976-77 Budget Instruc-
    tions, and Examples of Program Submissions.*

*A Survey on the Developments in State Budgeting,* conducted by the National
    Association of State Budget Officers; Systems, Techniques, and Data
    Committee (April 1975).